First Edition

MASTERING TRAINING AND FACILITATION SKILLS

The Training Intelligence Handbook

Azizullah Bangash

ISBN: 9798575907565
Imprint: Independently published

Cover design by: Azizullah Bangash
Library of Congress Control Number: 2018675309
Printed in the United States of America

DEDICATION

To my parents, brothers and sisters this
book is affectionately dedicated. I also
dedicate this book to amazing people and
organizations I have worked with and my
Center for Awareness Training and
Development team members who helped
me in the process.

BOOK CONTENT

AUTHOR MESSAGE

Inspiring your learners is an art and science which requires skills, knowledge and unique approach. Remember what really matters are how the training content is delivered to change the attitude of the learners and give them transformational experience. While working with founders, managers, entrepreneurs, trainers and teachers, I realized that their interaction with their team is not inspiring and effective, and they lack in understanding the needs or gaps of employees at work, and are not effective in developing their capacity to make them productive.

In today's world especially in post COVID19 scenario not only the trainers, managers or teachers need to develop effective training and facilitation skills both onsite and online but it has also been very essential for the founders, entrepreneurs and all working professionals who are leading team at any level to have effective and inspiring facilitation skills to make sure they inspire their teams, build their capacity and improves the overall organization capacity.

Mastering Training and Facilitation Skills – The Training Intelligence Handbook, is not only for the trainers, teachers and managers but it is also for founders, entrepreneurs and professionals who are leading a team and want to learn and enhance their training and facilitation skills. This book will help you learn how you can develop skills to be the best and be a very effective and inspiring trainer, team leaders, manager or founder that will in turn help your organization or client grow and increase its employee's productivity.

If you have any comment or suggestion, please do not hesitate to contact me on azizullah@catd.org.pk. I am excited to have you go through my book. While enjoying reading it, learn from it and apply the knowledge, skills and concepts. I wish you good luck.

Azizullah Bangash

INTRODUCTION

Mastering Training and Facilitation Skills – The Training Intelligence Handbook, has been designed for trainers, managers, entrepreneurs, teachers and professionals who are interested in developing inspiring and effective training and facilitation skills. These skills are very essential to make a strong team and to lead an organization to the height of success with the help of the team. This book will help you learn and understand the very essential details that are needed for the training of a team working for an organization. In this book, you will learn the most vital concepts and gain knowledge that will help you learn to design a framework for training your team. The skills that you learn through this book will enable you to become a great leader in your workplace. Keeping the fact in view that the success of an organization lies in how the leaders of a particular organization train their teams to guarantee their efficiency at work so that they achieve maximum productivity.

Not everyone can deliver effective training as it requires a lot of skills.

The book has been divided into seven sections. Section -1 covers concepts of training and development, and different between them, and in section-2 you will go through the roles and qualities. You will learn how you can design content in section-3. Section-4 will take you through effective communication and learning styles of the learners and in section-5 you will learn key facilitation skills. In section-6 you will go through designing training feedback and evaluating training programs. The book also includes section-7 which covers online content delivery due to the recent drastic shift to online learning due COVID19.

Each section has a different chapter dedicated to the most important area of training to help you understand it well and develop highly effective training and facilitation skills. This book will help you learn how you can develop skills to be the best and be a very effective and inspiring trainer that will in turn help your organization or client grow and increase its employees productivity.

SECTION 1

UNDERSTANDING TRAINING AND DEVELOPMENT

The targeted concepts in this section are training and development. Here you will learn all the necessary knowledge you need to have about training and development, and differences between them. Before learning how to train and develop a team for your organization, you need to learn what training and development is.

CHAPTER # 1

TRAINING & DEVELOPMENT

Training and Development in an organization is one of the essential activities to improve specific skills, abilities, and knowledge of the employees leading to the achievement of goals of the organization. Through these training & development programs, the organization tries to improve the employee's performance, so that the ability to perform increases. The employer attempts to enhance the skills through learning, mostly to change the employee's attitude or increase his or her skills and knowledge. Keeping in view the employee's performance and the deficiencies, short training & development programs are developed and conducted. For newly employed personals, the initial pieces of training are fundamental to know the organization structure and working methodology.

In most of the organizations, Human resource management is concerned with the development of specific training to be provided to individual employees. These training and development concerns with organizational activity aimed at the betterment of the job performance of individuals and

4

groups in organizational settings. After the shortcomings in performance are identified, a training program is arranged; thus, training and development can be described as the educational process that involves the sharpening of concepts, skills, changing of attitude and increasing knowledge to enhance the performance of employees. The field has gone by several names, including "Human Resource Development," "Human Capital Development" and "Learning and Development.

> *Development refers to some learning opportunities specifically designed to help employees grow.*

Training & Developments helps in the development of following aspects of an organization;

Productivity – increasing the productivity of the employees

Team spirit – in inculcating the sense of teamwork, team spirit, and inter-team collaborations

Organization Culture – It develops and improves the organizational health culture and effectiveness

Quality – Helps in improving the quality of work and work-life.

Morale – Helps in improving the confidence of the workforce.

Image – Helps in creating a better corporate image.

Profitability – It leads to improved profitability and more positive attitudes towards profit orientation.

Training and Development encompass three main activities - training, education, and Development;

- **Training:** Training is both focused upon, and evaluated against, the job that an employee currently holds.
- **Education:** This activity focuses upon the jobs that an individual may potentially hold in the future, and is evaluated against those jobs.
- **Development:** This activity focuses upon the activities that the organization employing the individual, or that the individual is part of, may partake in the future and is almost impossible to evaluate.

BENEFITS OF TRAINING & DEVELOPMENT

Specific and targeted training is one of the essential activities for organizational development, and successful training is indeed fruitful to both the employers and employees of an organization. The essential benefits of targeted and specific training are;

- Increased productivity

- Less supervision
- Job satisfaction
- Skills Development

The organization's performance can be increased via Training and Development programs, i.e., an Organization get more effective decision making and problem-solving. It helps in understanding and implementing the organizational policies. Training and Development help in developing leadership skills, motivation, loyalty, better attitudes, and other aspects that successful workers and managers usually display.

CHAPTER 2

DIFFERENCE BETWEEN TRAINING AND DEVELOPMENT

Training and Development are mostly used together, but there are significant differences in "training" and "development." Organizations knowing differences set priorities and strategies for Organization to HR development. Both training & development are essential for employers and employees whereas Organization is benefitted by both.

Understanding the Difference between Training and Development:

The difference between the two concepts should be kept in mind when discussing training or development:

- **Short Term vs. Long Term:**

Training is short term. The training course may be to improve the communication skills, a conference to explain a class to use the Excel application or the protocol for returning a product.

Development focuses on long term implementations. I.e., a strategy proposed to HR managers for implementation over a long period that is expected to bear fruit. This is a continuous process in which the Organization is trying to develop professionals for the next position of responsibility.

- **Job position vs. Professional career:**

Training is designed for a specific job post. It seeks to provide professionals with tools and skills, taking into account the work that they will be doing at the Organization. Training focuses on a job position.

The development puts emphasis on building a prosperous professional career. The objective of this is to get the best out of each professional in the Organization. Identifying and developing their skills in fields in which they can easily progress.

- **Specific objectives vs. Open objectives:**

Training is specific and well defined, teaching new protocols put in place by the Organization.

The objectives of development are always much broader and can cover all types of knowledge and skills. Development is less concreted, which often focuses on philosophical issues, changing habits, and improving skills.

- **Group vs. Individual:**

Training is a program designed by the Organization. An expert in the concerned field is hired to conduct training. For instance, training courses decide what sort of tools should be used, set guidelines to follow by employees during training activities. Training is usually provided in a group.

Development programs are personalized, the person who is ultimately responsible is the employee. The most critical focus is not on lessons taught by a tutor, but instead of the self-learning process and progress that must be taken on by the professional.

Training is a short term process, usually requiring guidance in a series of steps to gain a skill. Training is generally given to general employees of the Organization and aimed at a specific task or job role.

THE PURPOSE OF TRAINING

- *To provide the ability to undertake a task or job*
- *To improve productivity and workforce flexibility*
- *To improve safety and quality*
- *To develop the capability of the workforce*

Development is long term in nature & is the capacities of Managerial level employees are developed to improve their skills like developing relationships, often to improve leadership, etc.

THE PURPOSE OF DEVELOPMENT

- *Better knowledge*
- *Changing attitudes*
- *Increased capability and skills*

SECTION 2

THE TRAINER

In this section, you will learn about the trainer. What type of skills and qualities does a person need to be a trainer? It is necessary to know that a trainer is a person with a specialized set of skills that he uses to train his employees; we will discuss them all here. A trainer is the most crucial part of a training program as all responsibility is on him to conduct the training

CHAPTER# 3

UNDERSTANDING TRAINING FROM
LEARNERS PERSPECTIVE

Aims, main points, and objectives of the training are;

- Improving business activities
- Encouraging and motivating employees to work more efficiently, and educating them about work
- Increases the learning process and knowledge of organizational personals, which will be gained in a long time through experience
- Training also helps in developing and sharpening of skills
- The training helps an organization to improve the behavior, attitudes, and performance of employees.

Training is a developing process for teaching skills of leading, directing, and educating employees to perform proficiently and effectively. Training can simply be referred to as a process where employees' acquires-job related skills and knowledge. Training is provided to employees to build skills for immediate success and day-to-day running affairs.

Training can provide an individual's lifetime skills, which can be applied in a different setting,

**promoting self-confidence, effectiveness, and
wellness.**

The primary goal of training is to improve the organization's business. The cost of training can be of significance in any business via these training organizations that accomplish immediate success and lifelong satisfaction. Training to the employees can also be given to communicating technical details and relevant information for better use of particular techniques and technology.

TRAINING IS NOT EFFECTIVE WHEN:

When there is no proper plan, training is then not very useful. Training is just not a platform for a trainer to through which they share their own skills, knowledge and experience only. At the orientation of the training, a trainer starts with his/her own self or admires the smartness of the trainees, the training gets boring, and the trainees then just take it for granted and do not gain much from this type of training program.

The success of such a type of training is of no guarantee. Such a brand of training there is a communication gap not only between the trainer and trainee but also between the participants also for exchange their experience in the field.

As mentioned above if there is no proper agenda of training and training material available, almost on one will benefit from this training program.

"ALSO TRAINING IS NOT A ONE-SHOT PROJECT"

Training is a continuous and nonstop program; it's not just a one-time small project. Where newly employed employees are provided with the history and structure of an organization. Even these training can be productive, when trainees are provided in hard form organization structure, with history and purpose of the organization; provided printouts of their duties and other relevant information. If the trainer shares his/her own experience, that will be a plus point, this type of training will have a good impact. To improve the productivity of these employees, more extensive but targeted training programs should be arranged from time to time, which will not only guide them but also motivate them to perform better.

A practical training component in any program includes orientation, continuing education, and coaching, consulting, peer learning, skill-building, and many other forms of information sharing and teaching. A trainer should take responsibility for the learning process.

The important things for a trainer to inspire learners and deliver effective training are;

1. **Subject Knowledge**
2. **Effective Delivery and Speaking skills**
3. **Be Resourceful**
4. **Emotional Intelligence**
5. **Open to feedback and learning**
6. **Inspiring Story Telling skills**
7. **Develop connection with learners**

CHAPTER# 4

TRAINER ROLES AND QUALITIES

The role of a trainer is to develop skills & competency of the employee's performance in the organization. He/She has to communicate to trainees the goals to achieve the goals of the training in a professional but straightforward way.

A trainer has to carefully plan the training program by - Planning the training program - Schedule time for training sessions - Selection of proper training methods - Amiability of training material and relevant   documents - Conduct the training in a good environment and finally - Post-training evaluation session

A good trainer and facilitator should have some essential qualities which should be logical, good -planner, having enough knowledge and relevant experience regarding the subject training program, and should have communication and presentation skills. He/she should be qualified for making the training program fruitful not only for the trainees but for the organization.

During long training sessions, the trainer should be able to give appropriate breaks so that the trainees are fresh during the session; necessary aid material should be available like visual and audio, etc. The trainer should involve the participants and make the program highly interactive. The experienced trainer should share industrial case studies. At the end of the training session, the summary of the full training should be provided by the trainer, and finally the training evaluation should be conducted to find the impact of the training program.

QUALITIES OF A TRAINER

Persons having the necessary attributes are not sure about the qualities that make an excellent trainer. Some of these qualities are:

- **Knowledge:** Trainer should have great knowledge of his/her subject. It helps trainers respond to learners effectively to help them understand the subject under discussion in all aspects.
- **Soft Skills:** For delivering effective and highly engaging sessions, trainers need to have effective soft skills

including communication, presentation and speaking skills. This makes the content delivery highly engaging and effective.

- **Listening:** What really makes learners understand and learn well in the training is when the trainer listens to them, understand their needs and respond accordingly.
- **Resourcefulness:** Being resourceful at the training helps trainers respond to the different situations during the session which ensure smooth execution of the session.
- **Empathy:** Empathy is a quality by putting him/herself in the same situation as the trainees enable a trainer to point out personal difficulties encountered by him in similar learning situations.
- **Honesty:** Honesty is the courage to recognize personal strengths and weaknesses and to be frank about these aspects to the person being trained to benefit them.
- **Patience:** This is shown by complimenting progress, even if it is slow and refraining from the anger when mistakes are made.
- **Pace:** This is an external speed governor, which acts more to slow down than to speed up. It is far better to move slowly to attain complete mastery than to push for rapid and sloppy completion.

- **Purpose:** A good trainer conscientiously moves a group of learners along to a pre-set destination. There may be breaks, stops, and shifts, but the goal is always fixed on specific performance standards and levels.

- **Listening Ability:** The trainer must hear questions raised by trainees, and understand if the questions reflect other problems, which were not addressed by the trainer. He should encourage the trainees to ask questions, and satisfactory answers should be given.

- **Respect for experience:** If respect is given to the experience and qualification of seniors, they will learn more effectively. This will encourage more participation and activity by trainees.

- **Prestige:** A trainer should take great care of the respect of his colleagues in the organization. The training program will then be strengthened by its acceptance among older and experienced employees.
Engaging: Interactive and experiential learning helps trainees, learn well and go through transformations. Trainer should be highly engaging during his/her session and should make his/her session interactive and engaging.

- **Encouraging and Motivational:** One of the biggest needs of trainees is to motivate and encourage them. Trainer must appreciate the trainee's participation and efforts. This makes trainees more engaged and appreciated which makes them be fully involved in the process.

- **Flexible and Adaptive:** The training session or meeting may not go as planned. Trainer should be flexible and adaptive to the situations, respond and act accordingly to make sure of impact and learning outcome.

- **Technology Usage:** In today's world due to technological development, a lot has changed in the training and teaching industry. There are different tools, software's and equipments used in the training industry. Trainer should be used to relevant technological equipments and tools to make sure he/she delivers the session effectively.

SECTION 3

DESIGNING CONTENT

In this section, you will learn about how a trainer will design content for a training session. Content designing is a very technical part. The trainer needs to ensure that the content is relevant, what is the impact of the content on the audience. Content is one of the fundamental parts of a training session, if there is no relevant content, the training session will not be impactful.

CHAPTER 5

TRAINING NEEDS ASSESSMENT FOR CONTENT DESIGN

Training needs assessment (TNA) is for identifying the knowledge, skills, and abilities required by an organization to achieve its goals. Proper TNA can help an organization to direct resources to areas of an enormous demand. This TNA should address resources to fulfill organizational goals, improve productivity, and provide quality products and services.

An organizational needs assessment is an internal need assessment of the organization, i.e., what type of skills, knowledge, and abilities are needed, and on the other hand, what resources are available in the organization in the form of employed staff and other related assets. Keeping both aspects, the organization will evaluate the problems, gaps, and weaknesses to be removed. Thus training programs will be developed via TNA findings to enhance the strengths and competencies of the organization.

THE TRAINING NEEDS ASSESSMENT PROCESS

Organization Needs Assessment process will help decision-makers and stakeholders for critical occupational and performance requirements by the organization. In TNA the points to consider are;

I. **Stakeholders – to whom training will be provided**
II. **Training contents & requirements**
III. **The impact of the training on stakeholders**
IV. **Sustainability of the training**
V. **Training timings and venue**
VI. **Financial valuation**

Besides these points the stakeholders' interest and business demands may also be considered during the need assessment. With this assessment, the organization will be able to identify the areas of training, which eventually reduce unnecessary financial, human resource, and time costs. TNA finally can also predict the outcome of the performance.

Even keeping in view the points mentioned above, for successful TNA, the Trainer and his/her team should;

I. **Consider the organization structure**
II. **Find out the areas in which training is needed**

III.   Budget kept for the proposed training

IV.   Stakeholders capacity, educational & technical skills (if required)

V.   The goals that the organization wants to achieve

VI.   Designing a questionnaire for the assessment

VII.   Method of gathering data from different sources for the TNA viii. Selection of success measuring tools next stage

TNA is to get deeper into the organization structure like gathering HR-related documentation including but not limited to;

a)   Organization Operation Manual

b)   Job descriptions starting from the Head of Organization till low level employees

c)   Evaluation of employee's performance strategies with performance appraisals, especially of those employees for whom the training is to be developed

The TNA team has to make sure to gather as much information as possible, which can identify the problems, weak operational areas, the management & employees' coordination, environment, confidence level, and status. The purpose of this information gathering will be to find out the problems faced by the organization, and how to reduce or reeducate the same with training, with the questions of WHY, HOW, WHEN and WHERE, keeping in view the organization budget, needs, technical and HR resources.

After finding the problems, suggest a solution to the management. Discuss the issues and its solution with higher authorities and recommend training or workshop for the concerned management or employees, as necessary.

The final step of the TNA team is to design appropriate training, with all the necessary training materials, methods of training to be used, pre and post-performance evaluation strategies, techniques, and channels. The team should also put on papers how the training will address the particular problem, how it will be catered through the training, and what will be the expected outcome of the training, benefits to the organization and employees.

CHAPTER# 6

TRAINING FOUNDATION PRINCIPLE AND

OUTCOMES

There are few principles for training, which can be a cause for a successful and fruitful one. These principles include, but not limited to the below-mentioned one. The most crucial principle is to have a training need assessment, through which an organization can benefit from the report and assess;

- **The training course needed**
- **To whom the training is required**
- **How, When, and Where the practice should be conducted.**

Selection of a targeted training course with the aims and objectives to achieve is a key. Suppose if training is needed in the IT section and training on character building is given, it will have some impact, but the actual aim and object of the exercise will not be achieved. So the first principle, after the TNA report is to select an appropriate training course.

From the TNA, if required, a list series for training can be prepared. On the top priority, technical skills should be kept, because of lack of technical expertise, for instance, if an employee is supposed to prepare reports in excel and he/she does not know how to insert basic excel formulas in the already made report, he/she or those employees need skills development training to reduce this gap. This training will not only increase the knowledge of particular employees but be beneficial to the organization.

Especially for the skills training programs, it should be ensured that the capabilities of the trainee are being assessed before starting the training and also after it has been provided to measure the impact of the training and to what extent the objectives have been achieved. From this assessment, management can evaluate and decide for further training of the same level or advanced levels.

The organization should not use only the old principle of training, like developing presentations and providing related documents to the trainees in a hall and giving the lecture. It should use different methods like on job training, mock drills, online training programs, provide audio and visual lectures with example & illustration so that the intended employee may acquire more knowledge and experience, etc.

One of the principles is that the trainer informs the audience about the objectives and expected outcomes of the training.

LEARNING OUTCOMES

The need of learning outcome list is so that you can set goals for the training session. Before writing learning outcomes, the training developer has to keep some point on the table, which can be useful for developing the outcome list:

I. **What organization wants from the training?**

II. **What the participants accept from the training**

III. **What knowledge or skills are required to develop?**

IV. **What will be gained by the participants from the training?**

V. **What will be the reaction after the training of the participants?**

A simpler type of question can lead to developing fruitful learning outcomes.

The learning outcome is usually in the form of a list of case studies, which shows the impact of pre and post-training. The outcome not only leads to the direct impact of the training but also improving the upcoming training resources, planning, designing, timing. After the full case study or outcome results for a particular training program the organization is in a position of evaluating;

a. **The impact of the training on employees and organization business**
b. **What will be the shortcoming in training**
c. **Retaining or replacing of selection methods of training**
d. **Make changes in the training sequence**
e. **Use of different tools for the training**
f. **Tools to use for learning pre and post assessment methods.**

CHAPTER # 7

DESIGNING LEARNING CONTENT AND UNDERSTANDING AN EFFECTIVE CONTENT DELIVERY

For effective designing a learning course and developing particular training contents one has to consider that;

I.   Why the training is to be conducted

II. Who will be the participants of the training

III. What is the purpose of training

Before designing learning contents the training developers should thoroughly read the Training Need Assessment (TNA) and make quarries (if needed) for further clarification. From the TNA, he/she may consider the following points and keep in mind or write for reference so that the training and material are designed as per requirements. The training course and material designer needs to know;

   a. The employees training needs

   b. Learning Outcomes

   c. Survey regarding targeted audience suggestions

d. Assessing their knowledge and skill level

e. Technical skill needs assessment

f. Method of delivering training

g. Material to be used for referencing

h. How will the evaluation of training be conducted, before and after the training

i. Aims and objectives of the organization to achieve

j. Start and ending of the training sessions

k. Timings and refreshment breaks

l. How to achieve expectation and satisfaction level from the course to be designed.

A training designer asks, "Why is this training being arranged?". The purpose of the training is for improving performance or introducing new products or policies, or change in market strategies etc. The purpose of the training is very important for effective & proper course design for particular training.

For instance if the training purpose is to improve employee performance, mock drills may be arranged for practicing after the theoretically taught to the trainees. For example, a customer care unit at a Call Centre the employee is trained how to respond to a call. A call is made to him and see his response, while other learners watch at the same time. After this role is played, learners can give and receive feedback from members of the group.

The designer has to keep in mind, "Who is the audience for this training?" he/she has not only to consider the level of knowledge and skills but the audience culture, learning skills, positions in the organizations, i.e., Executive Level, Managerial Level, other levels. Design the course required as per different levels, educational & technical status, IT and Online learning capacity, etc. A good training program developer is one who also keeps in mind the age level of the audience, if it's of experienced and aged employees more like the serious and informative course will be considered, they usually don't prefer online or computer related training, instead prefer interactive face to face training, etc. On the other hand, the young audience prefers online, audio & visual lecture or illustration and one computer learning techniques. A final question arises, "What do your learners need to take away from the course?" This question is also very important since that will help in developing a list of what participants should know and should be able to do after they complete the course.

This will help not only in developing learning content but also the training delivery method, i.e. theoretical, mock drills, videos, audios or other delivery modes. Be as action-oriented as possible, and selective in mode of conducting the training. For example, if you are training an audience on how to build a house, learners must be able to read a blueprint, lay the foundation, measure materials, etc. You could also write a second list on what is "nice to know " — areas of knowledge or skill that you can add in if you have enough time. These lists will help you organize your content into a learning plan.

A designer can easily design an excellent training program and course material while keeping the points discussed in the chapter.

SECTION 4

COMMUNICATION AND LEARNING STYLES

In this section, we will emphasize the tools and techniques that make a learning process of the training session very effective and easily understood by the trainees. One can consider these the basic tools and techniques required in a training session. You will learn about what tools do you need in a training session and what techniques do you have to learn to make your training session fruitful.

CHAPTER 8

LEARNING STYLES OF LEARNERS

In the present world, there are different ways of learning and means but out of them, the most effective styles of learning are;

1. **Aurally/Lecture**
2. **Illustrational/Visually**
3. **Logically**
4. **Observational**
5. **Practically**
6. **Privately**
7. **Socially**
8. **Linguistic**

Most people use the learning styles mentioned above, which are usually developed in early childhood. It starts with observation, where a newborn baby starts learning by observing the actions being performed around them. Later on, he/she develops their learning by further adopting any one or more than one of these learning styles. It will be a good idea to explain the learning styles briefly for better understanding;

AURALLY/LECTURE

This type of learning style is usually through lectures or reading while listening to music or making some constant vibration or rhythmic actions.

ILLUSTRATIONAL/VISUALLY

This type of learning style prefers depiction for an explanation. For example, illustration, graphs, pictures, clip arts, which means learners feel comfortable and remember more efficiently with illustrations, photos, images, etc, are shown to them instead of being explained the concepts to them theoretically.

LOGICALLY

This type of learning style tries to put logic and reasoning to everything and evaluate mathematically. The more logical it is, the easier it is to understand and learn.

OBSERVATIONAL

As also mentioned above, it's the first learning style, and usually, most of the learners develop this style, i.e., observing different scenarios and gathering information and learning from it.

PRACTICALLY

This type of learning style prefers practicing, like assembling and disassembling a water motor with their hand. Learners can learn more with practical work rather than visually or theoretically explain to them.

PRIVATELY

These types of learners prefer to learn one-to-one from teachers or trainers. They usually don't grab more information or knowledge in a class or gatherings. Crowds get them distracted, and thus they need one-on-one learning style.

SOCIALLY

This type of learning style is based upon interactions, and learning in a social environment, via discussions, debits, sharing experiences with each other. They can retain more information about their subject training by sharing and exchanging views with co-trainee and trainer and vice versa.

LINGUISTIC

Linguistic or verbal learning is the one who learns information through reading, writing, listening, and speaking.

Mostly everyone has a dominant learning style or styles, through which he/she can learn more efficiently and quickly. However, one can easily adapt himself or herself to develop the ability to learn with a different method, other than the dominant ones. Further, it is very beneficial to develop using other learning styles other than dominant ones because of different circumstances and situations.

Research shows that using different learning styles is also suitable for our brain health because different styles use a distinct portion or area of the brain, which keep the mind active and in use. By involving more of the brain during learning, the remembering and learning process is more than the one adopted by our dominant learning style.

CHAPTER # 9

EFFECTIVE COMMUNICATION

In this chapter, we discuss the various channels through which one can effectively communicate with the trainees during a training session. There are four communication channels;

1. **Verbal**
2. **Nonverbal**
3. **Visual**
4. **Written**

VERBAL:

Communicating with the help of words and phrases is called verbal communication. In this type of communication, a person needs to use appropriate words and phrases. The best method of verbal communication is to use loud and clear words that are easy for everyone to understand.

Here listening to people is as important as talking.

NON-VERBAL:

Words alone might not deliver the message intended, gesture, tone and body language is another important channel of communication that plays a vital role in delivering your message. With confident body language, you can convince people that you are an expert, and people will trust you and learn from you.

VISUAL:

Another channel of communication is visual communication. People get your message through looking. You can carry out an activity in front of them to show them practically what you are trying to tell them. You can also depict your message.

WRITTEN:

People tend to understand the messages being delivered to them through written material. For this purpose, you can give them handouts that have a briefing of the training session. This way, they will be able to understand you better, and the training session will be more effective.

Following are some of the most important elements and aspects to understand and master to ensure Impact during presentation/communication;

Appearance

Physical appearance, i.e., outlook and body language, has the first impression on the audience.

Eye contact

A natural expression of interest with the audience is Eye contact, which is very important. **Posture**

The posture of the body and the tone of the speaker should be in coordination.

Vocabulary

A rich and varied vocabulary of the subject is crucial that will give the listeners a taste of the subject and choosing appropriate words.

Jargon

Avoid jargon. Unless, of course, you are in a specialist field, and the training consists of learning specialist vocabulary.

Gesture

The gestures need to be natural and spontaneous.

Space

The available space for the speaker should be used if and when desired.

Voice

A wide variety of information is picked from a person's voice, a general state of health, mood, social class, and what part of the country they come from.

Expression

We do not hear what our voice sounds like to others because it resonates in the bones of our skull.

Breathing

Vocal projection needs proper breathing.

Timing

Take time while talking, don't rush.

Congruency

"A blur of blinks, taps, jiggles, pivots, and shifts--- the body language of a man wishing urgently to be elsewhere." Use your voice congruently with your words.

Pauses

Pauses are the natural punctuation in what we say

Tonality

There are also the natural vocal inflections that can use to create effects. In communication tonality plays an important role in delivering your message.

Words

At last, the part we practice, shape, and fret over the most.

These all play key roles in delivering effective, highly engaging and impactful training sessions.

CHAPTER# 10

HANDLING DIFFICULT AUDIENCE

There are times and several reasons when the speaker faces a "tough audience." For instance, non-serious audience, audience not interested in the topic of the training, too much-experienced audience, either too high level or low level of audience or even trainees expecting other than the training being provided. Many more reasons can be quoted.

However, there are few key points to remember when presenting to a tough audience, which includes, but not limited to, and a good trainer usually shares the experience with co-trainers, the problems he/she has faced during the training.

The very experienced audience sometimes expects to gain new ideas or knowledge. In contrast, due to their experience, they find themselves in a situation that the training, which is being provided, is a waste of their time and resources. In such a condition, the speaker should apologetically express his view and point of their interest and listen to the audience and respond to the observations in exceptionally several manners, and if possible, change the style of his presentation for gaining their attention.

There are situations when the speaker expects to have an audience with some basic knowledge of the related topic. In contrast, when he/she starts a lecture or presentation, the audience doesn't understand, because of the lack of knowledge on the subject, in this situation, the speaker may not get frustrated or starts dishonoring the audience. Instead, he/she may come down to the level of attendance and put himself in their shows, and before this main presentation he/she may provide some background to what he/she is about to deliver in the upcoming topic of discussion. Arguing with the audience about their knowledge is not the right way of dealing with this type of demanding audience.

Sometimes the speaker faces a non-serious audience. This can be due to the topic, which is not of their interest or inappropriate topic for them, or an inexperienced audience. Many other reasons can be for non-seriousness. In such a situation, the speaker may change his/her presentation style to the tone, which may cause the diversion from non-seriousness towards attention towards the targeted information, which is the objective and aim of the training.

There are situations when the audience feels that too much information is being provided in a concise time, and they are not able to learn what they want from the course. So for this purpose, the speaker should accomplish the presentation in such a way that the audience is satisfied. If a few of the audience needs clarification by asking a question, it should be addressed and the points to be clarified. In this manner, the tough audience will get the speaker's attention and will also honor the speaker rather than teasing him.

Sometimes it's a good idea to ask a volunteer from the audience to help him out when they somehow don't understand the speaker's point of view due to the speaker's way of presentation or any other reason. In this way, the audience will be more attentive and involved in the training. In this situation, also the speaker should not be aggressive; instead, he should be very polite and make the audience feel that he has come to educate them in a friendly environment.

Overall it's a difficult task to make a smooth presentation to a tough audience but highly recommended that the speaker does not get flustered and overwhelmed, because of this the audience may also get frustrated. The training to be conducted will not be much effective as it should have been; so if the audience senses this frustration; and it will not result in an effective presentation.

A speaker should remain professional and find a way out of the problem, which can change the audience's behavior and make the training successful, not only for the organization but also for the trainees. Keeping in view the experience, the speaker should be prepared for the next presentation to give to a tough audience. Stepping outside of the presentation comfort zone becomes more comfortable with the practice. It makes the speaker a better and more confident presenter when sharing information or delivers a sales pitch to an audience that knows and loves the speaker.

SECTION 5

DEVELOPING EFFECTIVE FACILITATION SKILLS

In this section, you will learn how to develop communication skills. The techniques for improving your communication skills will be discussed. You will learn what the effective means of communication are since talking is not the only way of communication, body language, gestures, and other means are also included. Communication is an essential part of the training session. Good communication means that the trainees can clearly understand the trainer.

CHAPTER # 11

UNDERSTANDING FACILITATION AND ITS PROCESS

Trevor Bentley defines facilitation as: **"The provision of opportunities, resources, encouragement, and support for the group to succeed in achieving its objectives and to do this through enabling the group to take control and responsibility for the way they proceed."**

And Ingrid Bens defines a facilitator as: **"One who contributes structure and process to interactions, so groups can function effectively and make high-quality decisions. A helper and enabler, whose goal is to support others as they achieve exceptional performance."**

A person whose role is to guide others through a process to a practical result is known as the facilitator. A facilitator is expected to adopt or develop few qualities discussed in brief here – but not limited to these mentioned below; to achieve effective facilitation skills: He/she should be flexible and have a quality of accessing the situation, environment, and adaptability. This is the far most quality which has to be developed. With the quality, a facilitator can easily adjust with the audience and transfer the information or knowledge to the target audience with ease.

He/she should not be part of a party or group if there is grouping the audience. Usually, the audiences for training are from different areas or sectors or of different ages and might have affiliation with the relevant segment. In such a situation, the facilitator should not be a party to any one segment. He\she should treat all the segments equally and not support one of the groups. In this way, all the parties will give preference to the facilitator and adhere to his instructions. With the attenuate he/she can transmit the message or conduct the training efficiently and effectively.

One of the other qualities of a facilitator is that he/she does not fix the parameters for his facilitation. Like fixing a time or outline structure to follow, both parameters are preferred and a good one, but keeping in view the target group situation, some appropriate flexibility may be kept for altering. Still the main aims and objective of the training should not be compromised. The flexibility should not be too much, which may cause a diversion from the original topic or target.

A professional facilitator is not the one who goes through the presentation or lecture in one go. Rather, he/she has to recognize the dynamics of the group and their knowledge about the topic also keep in mind the technical or professional skills. A qualified facilitator makes the training a dynamic one; by putting questions and make the audience responsive in the way of replying or discussing the same in a group. This is one of the keys to unlocking the group's potential and also achieve the goal of training.

A facilitator's other quality should be to get the attention of the audience who are non-attentive. He/She can be done by pausing the presentation for a while and giving a smile or nod needed to intervene or indicate support or challenge to what is going on. This will be enough for getting attention.

There are situations; when the facilitator feels that the audiences are getting bored, they can offer a short break for a cup of tea, refreshers, energizers, Q/A etc.

Skills required to handle different situations are observation, listening, reading body language, understanding human behavior, exchanging experience with other facilitators and gathering other facilitators' ideas, and stepping out of the content. All these can be achieved through practice.

CHAPTER # 12

PRESENTATION, FACILITATION AND TRAINING SKILLS

Chief of the aim of the Presentation, Facilitation, and Training is to transmit particular information to targeted audiences. But still, there is a difference in the three categories, which is:

Training is to teach a specific skill to a person or a particular group. Before training is provided, the need assessment and analysis should be carried out to find out the gapes, and the basic course is designed.

On the other hand, facilitation is to provide training to people to deal with some problems and issues, without directly involving in the matter and without any mishaps. For facilitation information regarding the situation or issue to be discussed, they are gathered. Also possible suggested solutions to be kept in front of the group for discussion.

Presentation is to describe or explain a particular topic(s) to a group of people in a proper manner. For presentations, knowledge & research on the topic is essential. Working on a presentation, it might be tempting to include some training type activities. But in many presentations, the speaker does not have access to audience analysis, a critical piece of information in the training analysis.

Some common points which many be kept in mind before opting either one of the functions, i.e., training, facilitation or presentation are;

- The target audience should be relevant to the activity. It's not that a presentation is needed on some topic and training is arranged for some other topic and vice versa

- Usually, the activity with large groups gets more extended than the expected time limit, and the speaker or trainer or facilitator has a hard time controlling the large group. It's better for handling to conduct the activity in a small group. It's also better to avoid too many short breaks during events, if not necessary, as per program for large groups.

- Especially with large groups, too many activities may cause loss of time, and the speakers or trainer may rush through dozens of PowerPoint slides or lectures, and the audience may miss out on information, which might have been relevant. If the facilitator diverts from the main problem or issues, and the people become frustrated because they were expecting some results. It is advised to concentrate on the main activity, still keeping in view the audience's attention and involvement.

CHAPTER 13

KEY FACILITATION SKILLS

The facilitator is to facilitate not dictate. For this, a facilitator should be able to make the process easier and assist in adequate planning. He/she acts like a guide to help move through a process. There are few skills of competencies, which are needed to be a professional facilitator, to drive a group towards their objectives effectively.

A few of these skills include an active listener, having excellent communication skills, skills of understanding the complexity of the problem and possible solution, a good coordinator, a developing synergist, and an effective technique of questioning.

One of the skills of the facilitator is to listen and to be heard by the audience. It means that a facilitator has first to listen to the audience patiently, and he/she should maintain a body language that assures the physical presence by facing them squarely, making eye contact, keeping an open posture, and so on, with an open mind. Another skill of a facilitator is that he/she should possess excellent communication skills. He/She should ensure the focus of the audience on the topic and keeps the audience busy via communication skills, and should be able to keep the audience on track and not let them divert from a discussion on the main issue.

A professional facilitator has to build skills to understand the problem/issues and finding common goals and interests, shared values, etc. are few acts that are good for creating a relationship with a new group.

He/She should have skills of synergy and be able to remove any distractions in a group. It can be managed by open discussion arrangement, in a face to face meeting, in a familiar place of interest. The facilitator encourages sharing of views, respecting each other's opinions, reaching consensus, and brainstorming sessions. The facilitator should possess excellent probing skills through open and closed-ended cross-questions.

CHAPTER # 14

FACILITATOR KEY ROLE

The facilitator is to facilitate in solving a particular problem faced by a community in a specific area or group. To address common problems or issues, the facilitator has some essential duties to perform, which include: Find appropriate persons from the concerned group and constitute a group to find a solution to the common problem/issues in the community. He/she should select such a person from each group who is being heard, valued, and his decisions adhere to the group. The facilitator's other role is to keep close coordination with the members of this group. First, try to get an individual group point of view on the problem and suggested solutions.

After probing into the problem and the solutions, he/she should arrange a meeting in a place acceptable to all the groups. The facilitator is to act as a helper, not as a party to the problem. He/she can put on the table his discussion/findings with all the related parties on the matter and let the participants discuss the issue.

The facilitator may intervene in between if the discussion is going out, of course, or the debate is being diverted to other issues instead of the common problem for which it has been arranged. It is not the duty of a facilitator to enforce his suggestion. He/She should ensure that the discussion is not only a peaceful environment but also the beginning and end of the meeting on time.

The facilitator also has to ensure that abusive language is not being used by any of the group members, and the discussion progresses in a comfortable environment. The facilitator should try that the members reach a conclusion, which is acceptable to all the groups. His/her role is also to record the final discussion outcome or result, if possible, signed by all the members of the community. A facilitator can move the discussions along, but he/she should not directly head the group. He/she may refrain from leading the group. Not necessary, but if the members agree, the facilitator can ask volunteers for coordinating in different parts of a session, like sharing an opening session, introducing a focus on the problem, and also for checking-out from the session.

SECTION 6

TRAINING FEEDBACK AND EVALUATION

In this section, feedback and evaluation sessions will be explained. The necessary tools and techniques will be described along with how these sessions can be useful for you. You will learn how to measure the effectiveness of a training session through feedback and evaluation Feedback and evaluation sessions are very important to track your progress. This way, you will know if your training session has been successful or not.

CHAPTER # 15

DESIGNING AND CONDUCTING TRAINING FEEDBACK

Planning for evaluation is an important step. A designer should prepare and design the evaluation plan with the training program. A designer should consider the following main point while designing the tentative course plan.

First, go through the training needs assessment report carefully and make notes concerning the stakeholder need and requirements, organization necessities and its target, concerns of the organization, shortcomings or gaps to fill in, method for connection data, evaluation method, and questionnaire for training, also identify the medium to conduct the practice, and finally criteria which will be used for evaluation in the program. He/she has also to keep in mind the operational manual for the related job(s). Along with these points mentioned in a paragraph write notes of other points quoted in TNA to develop a good plan for the training.

This evaluation plan should also specify the what, where, and when, i.e., the program to be evaluated, the location of the program and its evaluation, and finally, the time for the program evaluation.

It should also specify the evaluation proposed and the questionnaire for evaluation. Means of the evaluation to be conducted should also be mentioned, i.e., how the information and what will be the sources for conducting the assessment. Mention the evaluation strategies and methods. The evaluators and evaluation customers should also be specified, i.e., who will be involved in the evaluation.

EVALUATION INSTRUMENT DESIGN

The most common four approaches and validity determining instruments are;

1. Content validity
2. Construct validity
3. Concurrent legality
4. Predictive validity.

Further, there are four procedures, ensuring that an instrument is reliable;

a. Test/retest
b. Alternate form
c. Split half

d. Inter-item correlations.

An evaluation instrument should also be easy to administer, brief and straightforward, and be economical.

DATA COLLECTION

Data can be grouped into two broad categories;

- Hard data may be desired but not always available
- Soft Data is used. Anyone of the methods may be used to collect the data.

The final essential and critical step is communicating the evaluation results/report. The various target audiences should be considered, and emphasis should be placed on the top management group. A standard format for a detailed evaluation report should be used to promote consistency in communicating results.

CHAPTER # 16-

TRAINING MONITORING AND IMPACT EVALUATION

Monitoring and Evaluation is a continuous process for monitoring any activity, especially training – its impact is on the employees as well as the business. It is a means by which an organization ensures that they have a competent workforce and will reassure regulatory bodies. Future needs of the organization can also be assessed by the outcome of monitoring and evaluation information. It can also be used from going forward, and the need for new training for learning and development opportunities is clear from the outcomes of the monitoring and evaluation reports. Both short terms and long terms approaches are necessary for Monitoring and Evaluation.

The overall impact and outcome from training are measured through monitoring and evaluation assessment of performance. Monitoring and Evaluation also help to identify areas to provide further improvement through learning and development opportunities along with which members of the workforce need more attention and training and how will you manage it.

The learning outcomes should be incorporated into the organization's regular business activities. These outcomes of Monitoring and Evaluation should be discussed on different platforms like;

    a. Supervision

    b. Case discussions

    c. Annual appraisals

    d. Observation of workplace

    e. Team meetings

Some of the lasting changes that can be led by the outputs of Monitoring and Evaluation include;

    I. Further development of specific learning interventions and training sessions

    II. Updating protocols & procedures

    III. Practice workshops and seminar

    IV. Organization strategic/business plan development and also an ongoing review of operations

    V. Discussions, debate and challenge at senior level

    VI. The impact of Monitoring and Evaluation is a continuing process

VII. The practice of the effects of learning should be followed up by the line managers, supervisors via staff supervision, team meeting etc.

VIII. Audits of practice to incorporate the impact of learning

IX. The reports of all M&E findings should be shared with future learning and development programmers so that they know where to put more efforts in order to increase the productivity of an organization.

Both qualitative and quantitative data has a place in learning and development impact measuring. Some examples of the types of evidence that can be used are: - Referral rate - Better recording - More detailed referrals/notes - Increased awareness as evidenced by what is being done and said - Fewer errors - Increased confidence - Safer practice - Increased number of practitioners attending training and development appropriate to their role - Programmers run at full capacity with learning outcomes achieve - Positive evaluations from delegates - Staff development embedded in the appraisal process - Positive findings on practice as shown via audits for example

In short, the Monitoring and Evaluation has a massive impact on every single field of the organization. A clear path can be made for the development of the organization with the help of the monitoring and evaluation reports since the authorities know where the shortcomings are and which steps are necessary for increase in the productivity of the organization.

SECTION 7

ONLINE CONTENT DELIVERY

In this section, effective online content delivery concepts and tools have been discussed. Due to Technological development and Covid19 more focus is on online meetings, classes and training. You will understand challenges of e-learning and checklist for delivering online sessions, and effective management of online class.

CHAPTER # 17

ONLINE CONTENT DELIVERY

Technological advancements and Covid 19 crises have proved to be one shifting the concept of training and development to a virtual learning. Especially the transmission of Covid 19 compelled most state governments to shift from the traditional learning system of a study/training place where trainers'/trainers' and trainees'/trainees' physical presence is compulsory to a virtual class system, i.e., online learning. To reduce even this small spread, meeting virtually is recommended. This will help reduce the spread of the virus and reduce the impact of Covid 19 on the businesses of the world.

Most businesses are being shut down across the world due to the Covid 19 virus. The remote digital platform is adopted by most of the businesses and schools for their meetings and teachings.

One research shows the increased retention of information's have been noted; meaning the change from the conventional meeting system might be converted mostly to the e-learning system due to the coronavirus.

This sudden shift from the conventional education system to virtual learning will be suitable for future adoption or revert to the regular system during post-pandemic times.

The online session is challenging, which is faced both by the audience and meeting conductor/trainer.

All the people are generally facing the following challenges in the e-Learning system.

ADAPTABILITY TO E-LEARNING

Adaptability is the first far most problem being faced by both the audience and the trainer. To transform trainees' and trainers' mindset is a difficult task, especially for those trainees and trainers who don't use the technology of e-learning. For them, this is 100% new technology and teaching system. This environmental change from the conference room system to the virtual class system is difficult for the audience of the training session as well as the trainer.

E-LEARNING TECHNICAL ISSUES

Another issue in the e-learning system is its technicality. Most of the trainers and trainees are not used to technical problems. Trainers face technical software and need to be trained for using different software for live streaming and recordings, for practical use to specialized software. On the other hand, the trainees also need some guidance for taking full advantage of using the e-learning software, and who to ask questions or clarification if he/she does not understand the lecture.

MOTIVATION:

Adopting a new system is not an easy task. During the initial stages, the trainees lose hope when they cannot understand the lesson, mostly the young. They have to be motivated by their trainer. This motivation is a must for continuing the training session; otherwise, if he/she loses this hope, they might quit training.

DISTRACTION

It is advised that during this training time, both the trainers and trainees avoid distraction. They should make sure that they are in a place where they won't get disturbed. This way, trainees can focus and actually learn from the training session, while the trainer will be able to train his trainees properly.

FEEDBACK / COMMUNICATION

The communication between the trainer and trainee should be regular. The trainer may take feedback from the trainees regarding the style of teaching method or support material to be provided. It means that the feedback and communication should be strong and regular.

VIRTUAL ENGAGEMENT

The trainers are to provide the trainee with reading material, assignments, PowerPoint presentations, etc. This task is carried out by using live chats, email, live session deliverables, etc. Some of the trainees find it difficult as compared to the traditional system.

These trainees are advised to directly contact their respective trainers in person or through a call or other communication channels like social media, etc., for clarifications and understating the lesion.

Here we have mentioned a few common issues the trainers and trainees face for adopting the new e-learning system. In contrast, there can be more issues faced by trainers and trainees individually.

CHECKLIST FOR ONLINE CLASS:

The trainers and trainees are required to prepare a checklist and ensure the availability of all the required items before starting the training session.

For trainees, the checklist should be;

- **The computer is in working condition**
- **Internet availability**
- **A notebook with a pen for taking notes**
- **Relevant subjects notes and other helping material**
- **Before the time of class, sign in or log in to the software**

For the trainer, the checklist should be;

- **The session's learning material is available**
- **Recorded lecture, presentation, or related material is open or on the computer's desktop for ready reference**
- **The computer is in working condition**
- **Internet availability**
- **A notebook with a pen for taking notes or a recorder for recording any quarries and questions by the trainees to respond later, which may not be left un-address or un-attended**

- **Sign in or log in to the learning panel from where the lecture is to be delivered.**
- **This list should also include the list of trainees in the training session for the record**
- **Write any other relevant item needed during the session.**

EFFECTIVE ONLINE CLASSROOM MANAGEMENT

It's easy to manage the trainees in the physical classroom. Still, it can be tough to control the disturbed trainees, i.e., delivering lectures online and creating a supportive learning environment. A study shows that managing virtual classrooms is not impossible, but to use some different techniques to control and manage the virtual training sessions.

Research shows that there are five most essential steps to effectively manage online training sessions or meetings. These five steps include the following but are not limited to these management steps; more practical steps and measures can be taken. These are considered to be the basic one.

1. Testing of Technology in use

2. **Criteria of Involving Trainees in the virtual classroom**
3. **Engagement of trainees during the session**
4. **Small-Group Sessions are conducted rather than a large number of trainees at a time.**
5. **Initially slow start of a session is recommended**

It's easy to manage the trainees in the traditional learning system, even giving a small warning, but this is not possible in the virtual classroom. The trainee may leave the session, or full course as this has been made very easy. In some cases, a trainee may just log in to show their presence and logout at the end of the session. It's better to motivate and encourage the trainee to take the class, and they should be kept engaged somehow by giving the short assignment, asking questions, or taking their questions and addressing them. It means that these trainees should be kept engaged and active during the class session. Still, it's not an easy task for a trainer to control or manage the disbursed trainees.

To effectively manage an online classroom, the trainer must first test the technology that is being used for conducting the session before taking the class. This is important because if the system is not working properly, the trainees get irritated, lose their patience, and leave the session if the session is live. The trainer is also advised to learn the Learning Management System and to test it before using it.

In the virtual training session, the trainees usually don't care about the class's dressing and norms, which is irritating for most trainers. Trainees don't give much attention to the lecture; if they live, they do make different types of disturbance during the session. It is highly recommended that in the first one or two sessions, the trainees may be asked to make a list of norms they suggest for the online class. The trainer then compiles the same plan and conveys the almost final norms to the trainees during the online session. This means keeping the trainees motivated and also caring about their suggestions, due to which finally, most of the trainees will abide by and keep up with the norms to some extent.

Some scholars also recommended that a large number of trainee classes be avoided and a small number of trainees grouped in a session.

To gather the trainees' attention in a session, the trainer should start the session very slowly and try to attain the attention and engage the trainees. When the trainer is sure that he/she has got the attention, then he/she should

adequately start the session. If the trainer starts the session quickly, some trainees may not correctly follow the lecture.

FINAL REMARKS AND FURTHER READINGS

I am hopeful that Mastering Training and Facilitation Skills –
The Training Intelligence Handbook, provided you some very
helpful and effective tools, concepts, knowledge and skills,
and key elements of training and facilitation skills and
capabilities with which you can become an inspiring and
effective trainer/facilitator, a manager, a teacher and an
entrepreneur who is able to inspire his/her team, and make
every team member or employee productive, efficient and
effective at work.   There are different concepts and
approaches in delivering effective training but the tools and
techniques explained in this book are based upon my
experience, expertise, knowledge and research which may
vary from the experience, expertise, knowledge and
research of other Consultants and Trainers. This book covers
many areas of expertise training and one may not be master
of all these tools, concepts, skills and techniques.

There is a lot more to explore about the training and
facilitation skills. While writing this book I came across
following books that are very helpful as they cover a very
broad range of areas of training and facilitation skills. I have

also used some of these concepts, skills, and approaches in designing my workshops and therefore these also have been very helpful when writing this book.

a. Bob Pike: **CREATIVE TRAINING TECHNIQUES HANDBOOK**

b. Ton de Graaf: **HOW TO BECOME A COACH and Build a thriving Practice**

c. Center for Awareness Training and Development: **TRAINING OF YOUNG TRAINERS – Trainer Manual**

d. United Nations Office on Drugs and Crime - Regional Office for South Asia: **GUIDE FOR TRAINERS**

ABOUT THE AUTHOR

Azizullah Bangash has eight years of experience in learning and human capital development, organization development, training and facilitation, entrepreneurship ecosystem and enterprise development; working with non-profit, for-profit, SME's, Academic institutions, and public sector organizations. He has worked with national and international organizations and being part of global communities, his experience and contributions have impacted young people, entrepreneurs, professionals, and organizations in Pakistan, the United States of America, the Republic of Turkey, and Kenya.

As a Training Consultant, Aziz Ullah helps organizations design strategies and programs for their greater impact, and facilitates learning programs nationally and internationally for corporate, non- profits, academia, and youth to enrich their leadership values, organizational impact, team performance, and productivity. National and Global

80

Organizations and Institutions engage him in different workshops, and programs as speaker and trainer.

In his professional career, he has designed and delivered multiple high impact learning and development programs and has worked with more than 60 organizations. He has executed and facilitated more than 400 learning and development programs, summits, and projects with/for partner organizations. He recently worked as an Organizational Development Fellow at The Resolution Project Inc. New York USA. He is currently serving as a Co-Founder and Director of Programs at the Center for Awareness Training and Development where he previously served as Co-Founder and Program Manager. He is also working as a Community/Lead Trainer for Facebook Community Boost Program Pakistan.

He is passionate about contributing in the field of human capital development, learning and organization development, training and facilitation, entrepreneurship ecosystem, enterprise development. He is a graduate of MBA (HR), B.Sc Civil Engineering, and a Certified Trainer.

Printed in Great Britain
by Amazon